BETWEEN MARS AND ME

A one-act drama by
Rose Helsinger

www.youthplays.com
info@youthplays.com
424-703-5315

 ISBN 978-1-62088-765-3.

COPYRIGHT RULES TO REMEMBER

1. To produce this play, you must receive prior written permission from YouthPLAYS and pay the required royalty.

2. You must pay a royalty each time the play is performed in the presence of audience members outside of the cast and crew. Royalties are due whether or not admission is charged, whether or not the play is presented for profit, for charity or for educational purposes, or whether or not anyone associated with the production is being paid.

3. No changes, including cuts or additions, are permitted to the script without written prior permission from YouthPLAYS.

4. Do not copy this book or any part of it without written permission from YouthPLAYS.

5. Credit to the author and YouthPLAYS is required on all programs and other promotional items associated with this play's performance.

When you pay royalties, you are recognizing the hard work that went into creating the play and making a statement that a play is something of value. We think this is important, and we hope that everyone will do the right thing, thus allowing playwrights to generate income and continue to create wonderful new works for the stage.

Plays are owned by the playwrights who wrote them. Violating a playwright's copyright is a very serious matter and violates both United States and international copyright law. Infringement is punishable by actual damages and attorneys' fees, statutory damages of up to $150,000 per incident, and even possible criminal sanctions. **Infringement is theft. Don't do it.**

Have a question about copyright? Please contact us by email at info@youthplays.com or by phone at 424-703-5315. When in doubt, please ask.

CAST OF CHARACTERS

ROLAND, male. In college. Suffers from severe depression and paranoia.

JAIME, female. In high school. Roland's sister.

Productions may change the characters' genders. If so, please update gender references as necessary (e.g. "he" to "she").

SETTING

December, 2001. An overcrowded, unclean apartment.

PRODUCTION HISTORY

I started this piece in the annual Play In A Day event with Beth Marshall Presents, where twelve playwrights come together to write short pieces in twelve hours that are performed the following night. My piece was directed by Chris Yakubchik, and featured Cody Moss and Bennet Preuss. I expanded the short two-page script into a full one act for District 5 Thespian Competition where it won Best In Show. It was later staged at Boone High School's New Works Festival where it was directed by Sofia Deler, with myself as Jaime and Matthew Roman as Roland.

ACKNOWLEDGMENTS

An immense thank you to my family and friends for their endless encouragement and insight. Thank you to Beth Marshall, and all of my original Play In A Day team. Thank you to my theatre teachers for providing their students meaningful opportunities to grow as artists and as people. And thank you to Sofia and Matt for believing in this script and bringing your whole hearts to the production. This script would not be possible without you.

SCENE 1

(The second Tuesday in December. Roland's apartment.)

(Lights up on ROLAND reading from War of the Worlds *by H. G. Wells.)*

ROLAND: "No one would have believed in the last years of the nineteenth century that this world was watched keenly and closely by intelligences greater than man's and yet as mortal as his own; that as men busied themselves about their various concerns they were scrutinized and—"

(JAIME enters.)

AH! God.

JAIME: Sorry, I didn't mean to—

ROLAND: You scared me there. You didn't—um, knock. You usually knock.

JAIME: You gave me a key. Remember? I let myself in.

ROLAND: Will you knock next time?

JAIME: Sure.

ROLAND: I'm just scared of being crept up on.

JAIME: Yeah, I know. Look, I brought you more food.

ROLAND: Can I check first?

JAIME: I promise I'm clear.

ROLAND: I know you are.

JAIME: Then there's no problem.

ROLAND: But there's a chance they infected you and you don't know.

JAIME: The Martians did not—

ROLAND: Please, for me. Can I check?

JAIME: Fine.

(Roland feels for a lump at the back of Jaime's neck and spine.)

ROLAND: Clear.

JAIME: What are you even looking for?

ROLAND: Their eggs implant themselves under the skin. Like a botfly. They use you as a human host until they're ready to hatch out of you.

JAIME: How do you know that?

ROLAND: I checked out this tape from the university library a while ago. They show a botfly burrow itself into the gut of a cow. I think there's a link between that species of botfly and the Martians. If I can figure it out, then we can unlock the key to their reproduction.

JAIME: That sounds big.

ROLAND: Colossal. It's extremely important and delicate research. I'm watching the tapes I have. Reading my book. Searching for connections. I'm also working on my computer monitor. I've been rewiring it and making changes to the mainframe, I think I can get it to run faster on a smaller platform.

JAIME: That's really good, the computer stuff. I'm glad you're working.

ROLAND: Of course I'm working. This kind of research and the theories I have on processors, if they turn out to be accurate, could revolutionize how we think about computers and what they could be capable of.

JAIME: You don't know how much of a relief it is to hear you say that. If you make some sort of breakthrough then I can show your professor. Your friends from school really miss you.

ROLAND: Please, don't lie to me. I know they're dead.

JAIME: Right. I didn't mean to upset you.

ROLAND: It's okay.

JAIME: I brought more food.

ROLAND: Thanks.

JAIME: Should last you through the week, yeah?

ROLAND: There's more than enough. You really don't have to do this for me.

JAIME: I do. I mean, I want to.

ROLAND: It's dangerous getting this stuff.

JAIME: It's the soup aisle, Roland.

ROLAND: Don't joke. It's not funny.

JAIME: Okay. You know, I can bring more than canned food.

ROLAND: No, this is plenty. You scavenge enough.

JAIME: I'm serious. I can pick up that coffee cake you like, the one that comes in a box.

ROLAND: What did I say about jokes?

JAIME: I bet there's at least one left.

ROLAND: There's not. Food like coffee cake has expired by now.

JAIME: I don't think so. I think that if you can bring yourself to ask me for coffee cake, then I'll get it.

ROLAND: I don't believe you.

JAIME: Level with me here. If you'd just try, then, I don't know. Maybe there's a chance if I came by with Mom's cake you'd actually accept it.

ROLAND: Don't talk about her.

JAIME: You know, she bakes nothing but that now. I come home and there's a fresh cinnamon coffee cake sitting there on the counter, and she's already cracking eggs for the next one.

ROLAND: That's not true.

JAIME: She keeps handing them to me every week I come see you. She says, "Give this to your brother, Jaime. It's his favorite." But I can never get them to you, can I?

ROLAND: That's not fair.

JAIME: The last time I brought one over you flipped out. You said it was an alien trick.

ROLAND: It was.

JAIME: You kept screaming, just screaming—it wasn't even words. I thought you were going to hurt yourself—or me.

ROLAND: I would never. But the Martians? They will climb into your skin and eat you from the inside out if you don't stay here with me, where it's safe.

JAIME: How would you get food then?

ROLAND: I don't know, but we'd figure it out. The world out there is dangerous, and it's only a matter of time before they get you and you stop coming back. You'll just disappear all of a sudden, and I'll never know how you died—only that you're dead.

JAIME: Look at me. I'm not leaving you. I'm not dead. Everything is going to be okay.

ROLAND: I don't believe you.

JAIME: I'm sorry.

ROLAND: It's not your fault.

JAIME: It is. I brought up Mom. I won't talk about her anymore.

ROLAND: Thank you.

JAIME: Don't think about it, okay? If that's easier for you, then, just don't think about what's out there.

ROLAND: Okay.

JAIME: Do some breathing, all right?

ROLAND: All right.

(Jaime breathes in for a count of eight and Roland joins her on the exhale for another count of eight.)

JAIME: Yeah? Now, on your own.

(Roland breathes in and out each for eight counts.)

Better?

ROLAND: No.

JAIME: At least a little?

ROLAND: Yeah.

JAIME: All right then. You got your breathing, you got lots of food, you're going to be fine.

ROLAND: Jaime, don't leave.

JAIME: I'll be back next week. Like every Tuesday.

ROLAND: Can't you stay a little longer?

JAIME: I've got a curfew.

ROLAND: Don't go.

JAIME: I have to. Mom needs—I mean, I have to.

ROLAND: Come back then.

JAIME: I will. Keep working on the computer. I'll see you soon.

(Jaime exits.)

ROLAND: Okay. Okay.

(He begins breathing like Jaime taught him.)

(Lights down.)

SCENE 2

(The third Tuesday in December.)

(Lights up on Roland reading from a copy of War of the Worlds.*)*

ROLAND: "It seemed indeed as if the whole country in that direction was on fire—a broad hillside set with minute tongues of flame, swaying and writhing with the gusts of the dying storm, and throwing a red reflection upon the cloud scud above. Every now and then a haze of smoke from some nearer conflagration drove across the window and hid the Martian shapes. I could not—"

(Jaime knocks at the door. Roland lets her in.)

ROLAND: Thanks for knocking.

JAIME: Of course. I have food.

ROLAND: Thank you.

JAIME: I tried to call you to tell you I was going to be late, but it wouldn't go through.

ROLAND: I unplugged the phone.

JAIME: What?

ROLAND: Someone tried to call me and I was afraid they were tracking me through the landline. They could use a tone to brainwash me.

JAIME: How long ago was that?

ROLAND: Maybe two or three months ago.

JAIME: You've had the phone down all this time? Oh my God, what if something serious happened and I couldn't get ahold of you? I can't believe I didn't call you until now.

(Jaime climbs behind the couch to fix the landline.)

ROLAND: Don't plug it back in.

JAIME: I'm not. I'm just fixing the wires so you don't set the place on fire.

ROLAND: Okay.

JAIME: Hey, did you work on the computer since I was here?

ROLAND: No. It's not worth it. The electricity will go out for good soon, and it won't matter what theories I have or what improvements I make.

JAIME: That's not true. You went to NYIT for the computer program. That's the whole reason you're here.

ROLAND: Things are different now. I just want to read.

JAIME: That book again. It's so banged up.

ROLAND: It's not really.

JAIME: Buddy, the pages are falling out. I'll buy you a new copy.

ROLAND: There aren't any new copies.

JAIME: Don't do this.

ROLAND: Come here—I need to check you.

JAIME: I'm fine. I promise, I'm fine.

ROLAND: Let me check.

JAIME: Don't.

ROLAND: It'll only take a second. Just hold still.

JAIME: Don't touch me.

ROLAND: Okay, okay.

JAIME: I'm sorry I snapped at you. I'm just really tired.

ROLAND: What's wrong?

JAIME: Nothing.

ROLAND: I'm not stupid. What's wrong with you?

JAIME: It's this pre-calc test on Thursday.

ROLAND: That's it?

JAIME: I already have a D in the class, so, I'm gonna be up for the next two nights studying. And I was already up all night last night, and I don't think I even understand what I'm cramming in my head.

ROLAND: A math test has you this freaked out.

JAIME: Not all of us can be born trig geniuses.

ROLAND: Is trigonometry what you're struggling with?

JAIME: Don't gloat.

ROLAND: I'm not. I skipped to calculus, but I think I can explain the basics. What section do you not understand?

JAIME: All of it.

ROLAND: Do you have any homework or a textbook I can look at? I'll go over it with you.

JAIME: You'd really do that?

ROLAND: Of course.

JAIME: You don't have to.

ROLAND: What else are born trig geniuses for?

JAIME: Thank you, oh my God, thank you. Here, I have a study guide in my backpack somewhere.

(As she rummages through it, Roland reaches over to check her neck.)

JAIME: What is wrong with you?

ROLAND: I had to make sure.

JAIME: So you lied to me?

ROLAND: You were the one lying about still going to school. Do you think I'm dumb? I would never fall for a Martian trick like that. If you were infected then—

JAIME: That's it. I will see you next Tuesday.

ROLAND: You're being unreasonable.

JAIME: Do you have any idea how hard it is to stay patient with you? You come at me with your apocalyptic garbage everyday, and you never ask me how I am, or how school is, or say thank you. I have to ride the subway from Brooklyn to get here. I only have one day off practice a week and I spend it with you. Do you know how much crap the other girls on the soccer team give me for that? Do you know how much Mom gives me for that?

ROLAND: Don't.

JAIME: She asked me four times today when you're coming home. She's out of her mind worrying. She thinks staying in Manhattan and being so close to all this is bad for you. It is bad for you.

ROLAND: I don't want to hear this.

JAIME: She says I'm enabling you. And she's right, I mean, I am.

ROLAND: You're not.

JAIME: I can't keep lying to her for you. That's the only reason she hasn't broken down that door. Because I keep saying that every week you're getting better, that you're almost there, that you're almost ready to see her.

ROLAND: I can't see her.

JAIME: Because you know she wouldn't play along like I do.

ROLAND: Because she's dead.

JAIME: That's really easier for you to think isn't it? You want Mom to be dead.

ROLAND: I don't want any of this to have happened. But it did. And it was real. I saw them, the Martians. They lit those buildings on fire. It was their invisible heat ray, just like in the book.

JAIME: God, I need to go home.

ROLAND: The aliens got you, didn't they? Didn't they?

JAIME: There aren't any aliens. They aren't real. All of this is in your head.

ROLAND: You're lying. They got to you.

JAIME: You've been here for almost three months. Mom wants you home. We want you home.

ROLAND: This isn't you. The Martians snatched your body out there where it's all burned to nothing. They implan—

JAIME: You're behind on your rent, your bills are piling up, you're flunking out of school—is that what's keeping you here? Every second you sit here it just gets worse. That's what's real.

ROLAND: Everything's gone. Everyone's dead.

JAIME: Two buildings, Roland. That's all it was.

ROLAND: No, I watched it from my window. I saw this huge pillar of smoke and these little dark shapes falling out of high windows faster than paper could fall and maybe they were just office chairs, but there were so many, and they weren't pieces of paper and they weren't chairs—they were people. They were falling or—or jumping out of the frying pan, but the frying pan was the fire and all they jumped into was the ground. I shut the curtains. I can't open them again. I can't leave my apartment; it's safe in here. Everything else in the world besides this room is gone. We are the only two people on earth.

JAIME: Here. I'll show you.

(She starts toward the window, which is the fourth wall. He tries to stop her.)

ROLAND: Jaime, no. I don't want see it all burned up. I don't want to see what's outside. No, you can't. It's all gone, it's all—

(Jaime makes a motion toward the audience like she's opening drapes.)

(A light brightens the stage the same way the sun would a dark room.)

JAIME: See.

ROLAND: It's there. It's all still. There.

(A breath.)

But the towers. Gone. I could see them from my window. Gone. Like God just picked them up and lifted them into the sky.

JAIME: No. I saw it on the news. They crumbled down on themselves.

ROLAND: What burnt them?

JAIME: Planes.

ROLAND: Oh. It felt real. Deep down I guess I knew it wasn't. But it made sense, somehow. To have the whole world be gone after something like this.

JAIME: But the world's not gone. Is that better or worse?

ROLAND: Both. How did people react? When they saw the buildings burning? What did they do?

JAIME: They started like this; everyone afraid, holding their breath. But then after weeks and months they. We. Could almost start breathing again. We went back to school. We walked down to the memorial. Then, slowly, we stopped wearing black. We walked our dogs down the street and bought coffees and complained about teachers and dates and movies. We danced at parties again. We lived.

ROLAND: They didn't. The people there. They didn't get to.

JAIME: Yeah. I know that.

ROLAND: It's all so messed up. It doesn't matter if you're good or bad or somebody's waiting for you or if you have kids, a family. Doesn't matter.

JAIME: I think it does. The way people remember you when you're gone.

ROLAND: What would you care what they think of you? You're dead. You don't care about anything—you can't. It's all nothing.

JAIME: I don't think so.

ROLAND: What?

JAIME: I think there's something.

ROLAND: Something?

JAIME: God—I mean God.

ROLAND: You can't be serious.

JAIME: I am. Mom and I, we've been going to church together.

ROLAND: Does that make you feel better?

JAIME: It's comforting. To know there's a higher power than us.

ROLAND: I'm glad you have that. You and Mom.

JAIME: You mean it?

ROLAND: Yeah.

JAIME: Praying helps the most I think. We pray for the dead, for their families, we pray for you too.

ROLAND: What do you pray for me?

JAIME: That you'll find the strength to overcome your fears. That the sadness in you will disappear.

ROLAND: It's not sadness. Sadness is easier. It's a feeling because of something specific: you cry because your grandma died, that's sad. This, what I feel, it isn't sad. It's heavy, like a weight right here between my chest and my stomach, and it's a comfortable weight. It's something you can sink into. A place where you just can't leave your bed because the weight makes you feel like right where you are, curled in on yourself, is the only place you're warm, the only place you're safe.

JAIME: We can get you back on your meds. They seemed to help.

ROLAND: They didn't. They weren't the right ones and I don't want to spend forever trying new combinations and strengths. I'm tired.

JAIME: I'm sorry. I don't know what to say. I think, maybe, I think you need to face it. You need to go outside. Maybe, today is—

ROLAND: I'm not going outside. I'm not—not there yet. I'm not sure I'll ever be there.

JAIME: That's okay.

ROLAND: I might never get better.

JAIME: Okay.

ROLAND: Don't leave. Stay with me.

JAIME: All right. I won't leave yet.

ROLAND: Don't leave.

(After a moment, Jaime begins to exit.)

JAIME: I'm sorry. I can't.

ROLAND: Please don't go, please—

(She's gone.)

(Lights fade.)

SCENE 3

(The fourth Tuesday in December, Christmas Day.)

(Lights up on Roland reading alone.)

(The curtains are shut again; meaning the previously lit section of the stage is back to the original dim.)

ROLAND: "They began to meet more people. For the most part these were staring before them, murmuring indistinct questions, jaded, haggard, unclean. One man in evening dress passed them on foot, his eyes on the ground. They heard his voice, and, looking back at him, saw one hand clutched in his hair and the other beating invisible things. His paroxysm of rage over, he went on his way without once looking back."

(The landline rings and he doesn't answer.)

JAIME: *(On the voicemail:)* Hey, it's me. C'mon, pick up. Sorry I lied to you about plugging the phone back in. Please pick up—I know you're there. It's not like you go anywhere else. But, um, maybe you're in the shower or asleep or something, so, I hope you get this message soon. Listen, I can't make it today. The snow is really bad, and the subways are super crowded with holiday traffic, and I'm really busy tonight, and I can't leave, so, I'm sorry. You should have enough food from the last time I was there, so, you'll be okay. Remember to do the breathing if you get freaked out. I promise I'll be there next week. Promise. Okay, I love you. Merry Christmas. Um, see you soon. Bye.

(Roland closes his book. Lights down.)

SCENE 4

(The first Tuesday in January, New Year's Day.)

(Lights up on Roland huddled in the corner. The curtains are still shut.)

(There's a knock at the door. Roland doesn't answer it.)

JAIME: Roland? I'm gonna let myself in, okay?

(Jaime enters. She has two wrapped presents.)

JAIME: Hey. I know you're mad at me.

ROLAND: You left me.

JAIME: I know.

ROLAND: You come every Tuesday. But you didn't come last week. You left me, you ran out and you didn't come back for a whole week.

JAIME: I'm sorry.

ROLAND: I thought something happened. I was so worried.

JAIME: I called.

ROLAND: Where were you?

JAIME: I went to a Christmas party.

ROLAND: That's it?

JAIME: It was at my boyfriend's house. He invited over the whole soccer team, all my friends. Oh—happy New Year.

ROLAND: I didn't know that. I didn't even know you had a boyfriend.

JAIME: You don't really ask.

ROLAND: I'm sorry.

JAIME: Sometimes when I'm with you, I feel like I'm losing my mind too.

ROLAND: Really?

JAIME: Like I'm watching you drown in a big tank and there's nothing I can do except bang on the glass and watch the bubbles come out of your mouth. And then when I leave, I start drowning too. I forgot what it was like to feel sane. To feel normal. I just wanted one night to pretend that everything was okay.

ROLAND: If I drown, it won't be your fault.

JAIME: That's not what I meant.

ROLAND: You should go.

JAIME: I'm not going anywhere.

ROLAND: If you want to leave, leave. I'll be fine.

JAIME: No, you won't.

ROLAND: I'm trying to do the right thing here, okay?

JAIME: I am not going to let you waste away in here.

ROLAND: That's not your choice.

JAIME: You live here. You live in this dumpster. Oh my God, your dirty clothes are everywhere, let me just—

ROLAND: It's okay.

JAIME: I'm just folding them. Let me put them in piles. I can clean them for you, like Mom does when you come home, only she really doesn't know how to use the dryer and ends up shrinking your clothes. But I do. You taught me how to do laundry, so, I can do it for you.

ROLAND: It's fine. The mess is fine.

JAIME: Where's your laundry basket? I can take it downstairs. The washing machine is in the basement?

ROLAND: It's okay if it's a mess.

JAIME: *(Grabbing the laundry basket:)* Oh here it is. You put so many newspapers inside. Do you mind if I dump it out? I promise I'll clean it up in a second. I'll start piling clothes in and I can have them clean as soon as the washer is done. Is there anything you want ironed? Here, I'll start organizing these newspapers so I can—

ROLAND: I can take care of it myself.

JAIME: It's okay, I don't mind.

ROLAND: No one is asking you to clean. I'm not asking you to do this.

JAIME: I know.

ROLAND: Do you?

JAIME: I like doing laundry. I'm good at it. The colors never run. I never forget to separate the white clothes. I always pick heavy wash on our machine for the twelve-minute cycle because it really scrubs the dirt out. I mean that's what you taught me.

ROLAND: Are you crying?

JAIME: No.

ROLAND: Jaime?

JAIME: Come home.

ROLAND: I'm not ready.

JAIME: Please.

ROLAND: You don't understand.

JAIME: What don't I understand?

ROLAND: That it wasn't far away for me. It was right there. I walked by those buildings every day. I had friends who worked there. A girl I went on a couple dates with. Guys from school. The woman who lived in the apartment above me. We would meet in the hallway, waiting for the elevator. She was so excited when she got that internship. She had a dog. This big, fat golden retriever. He hated being left alone, so he would make that pleading noise at her door until she came home from work. And after, her dog just kept whining. I could hear him scratching and howling above me. I convinced myself it was the Martians digging down to find me and eventually a neighbor must have taken him to a shelter or something. But he's a dog. He'll never understand what happened or why he'll never see her again. He's just a fat, dumb dog that'll keep waiting for her to come home. Tail wagging and tongue out. Any minute, he thinks. Any minute. You don't understand. You didn't lose anyone.

JAIME: I lost you. *(Beat.)* My brother cast a long shadow. He beat me at chess in every game we played. He never let me win. He cared about his grades and shaved every morning at six am. He baked coffee cake with Mom and delivered pizzas to help us make ends meet. I love my brother. I miss him. I don't understand what happened or why I might never see him again. I look at you and I see a ghost of him. I look at you and I wait for him to come home.

(Roland doesn't reply.)

Say something.

(Nothing.)

I don't know what to do. I thought when I opened the curtains and you saw people, the world, that you'd get better. You stopped talking about aliens and I thought it was over. But it's not and I don't know what to do. I tried to step up. Take care of Mom like you did. Take care of you. But I'm not you. I'm not strong enough. I'm doing the best I can, but I'm fifteen. Tell me what to do. Tell me how to help you.

(Roland remains silent.)

Fine. I can't do this anymore. I'm leaving. I'm sorry. Here's your Christmas present. I picked it out. This one's from Mom. She sends her love.

(Jaime walks to the door.)

I'm not coming back.

(Jaime exits.)

(Roland sits a moment.)

(He opens Jaime's present. It's a brand new copy of War of the Worlds. *Roland reads the ending aloud:)*

ROLAND: "And strangest of all is it to hold my wife's hand again, and to think that I have counted her, and that she has counted me, among the dead."

(He opens the present from his mom. It is a homemade coffee cake. He stares at it and begins to fall apart.)

Jaime?

(No answer. He looks toward the door.)

(He gets up slowly and goes toward it. He hesitates before opening it.)

JAIME? Jaime?

(Jaime appears from the hallway.)

(Roland steps outside the apartment and into the hallway. He rushes to her.)

I'm sorry. I'm so sorry.

JAIME: It's okay. I've got you. It's okay. Do you see where you are? You're standing outside your apartment. You're safe.

ROLAND: Did you really mean it when you said you were never coming back?

JAIME: I didn't know what else to do.

ROLAND: You don't have to come back. But if you want to, bring Mom with you.

JAIME: Are you sure?

ROLAND: I can't promise I'll get better, but I'll keep trying.

JAIME: Okay. Hey, you're still here. Even after all this, you are still here.

ROLAND: I'm still here. We're still here.

(They hold each other. Lights down. End of play.)

The Author Speaks

What inspired you to write this play?

I was only two years old when 9/11 happened and hold no memory of the event itself. I've learned gradually about it over the years in school, from my parents, stories, accounts, movies, and plays. Numerous people lost parents, siblings, spouses, children, and all the others dearest to them. Another great many lost people they barely knew, or didn't know at all. As I listened to people's stories, I realized this experience wasn't as represented in the arts I'd seen. Whenever I asked someone about their experience with September 11th, they know exactly where they were, what they were doing, whom they called first, how it felt like the end of the world. They're extremely personal stories and tend to fall into the category of either, "I lost someone there," or, "I knew someone who lost someone." I became interested in writing a piece of theatre that didn't try to encompass the entire event, but instead focused on a single perspective like the ones I heard from others. I was sixteen when the Pulse shooting happened on the same street I grew up on. I know exactly where I was, what I was doing, whom I called first, and how it felt like the end of the world. I didn't lose anyone extremely close to me, but I knew people who lost people. I was awake when it happened, staying up all night to finish a library book, and I remember the group chat blowing up. Text after text of wild theories and worries, no one knew what was happening, just that we were afraid. Everyone was so confused and scared, full of despair and disbelief. I fixated on that moment when it felt like the world was burning down outside around us and the story began to take the shape of someone who was stuck in that initial stage of paranoia and anguish and couldn't escape it. I wrote this play as a representation of experiencing tragedy from the sidelines, how it can intensify other issues within our lives, and how we heal from that.

Was the structure or other elements of the play influenced by any other work?
The biggest influences on the script are ***Dancing Lessons*** by Mark St. Germain and ***Edith Can Shoot Things And Hit Them*** by A. Rey Pamatmat. They're my favorite minimal-cast shows, and I think it's amazing what these playwrights can do with just two/three people. In ***Edith Can Shoot Things And Hit Them,*** the way the father was omnipresent without actually appearing onstage strongly resonated with me when I read the script. To a lesser extent, I tried to capture that feeling with the mother in this play.

Have you dealt with the same theme in other works that you have written?
This is the first script I've written that tackles these specific issues. I've written about family and elements of grief before, but never a pair of siblings, which made this play especially fun and challenging to write. I noticed within the plays I read how rare it was to find a sibling relationship as the main focus. I have a younger brother myself and can identify with the particular struggles inherent in growing up with another person. The relationship between Jaime and Roland is so strained because they're taking on parental roles toward each other as siblings, which was interesting to explore as a writer.

What writers have had the most profound effect on your style?
Mark St. Germain's incredible dialogue is a peak I strive for. The way he captures the trauma and internal agony of a character in the perfect external way. Naomi Wallace's effortless embrace of the strange pushes me to think further outside of the box and not to be afraid to be wild and creative with my work. Steven King's book, *On Writing,* laid the

groundwork for my fierce love for storytelling and offered guidance that improved me greatly as a writer.

What do you hope to achieve with this work?
I hope to speak to and represent the experience of a tragedy affecting someone's life, from the perspective of not losing someone extremely close to them, but still feeling like the world isn't safe anymore. Roland's spiral downward is triggered by the events of 9/11, but all the issues he's dealing with existed before then, and are only exacerbated by that trauma.

What were the biggest challenges involved in the writing of this play?
The biggest challenge was cutting back the extraneous ideas that didn't serve the greater narrative. I had numerous extra scenes and whole plotlines that were cut because they distracted from the main points instead of adding to them. Killing my darlings was rough, but important to get the clearest script possible.

What are the most common mistakes that occur in productions of your work?
The most common mistake made in productions of my work is an unwillingness to make dialogue move. In dramas, it's easy to think that every moment has to sit with a pregnant pause on either side of every line. I encourage finding the moments where dialogue races back and forth. In arguments you spill over each other's speech, and sometimes speak without even thinking about what's coming out of your mouth. As important as the slow, heavy moments are, they're only powerful when other sections move like a ping pong match.

What inspired you to become a playwright?
David Lee, my theatre teacher during my sophomore year of high school, introduced me to Naomi Wallace. He taught us

about nonlinear plays and convinced me to buy a copy of Michael Bigelow Dixon's book, *Breaking from Realism*. I was just getting into literary fiction like Karen Russell's short stories, and I fell in love with how strange writing could be. I've known since I was twelve that I want to write fiction for the rest of life, and as soon as I began learning the secret sides of theatre, I knew I would write plays too. I discovered how unique a medium theatre is in the stories it tells. In class we read ***The Curious Incident of the Dog in the Nighttime***, and it revolutionized my ideas of what was possible in a theatrical space. I love playwriting because there are no limits on the stage, only your heart.

How did you research the subject?
I read a great many firsthand accounts and reflections from New Yorkers. I watched numerous videos of news coverage at the time and firsthand footage. There's one specific video taken from an NYU dorm that Roland's monologue is based on when he's talking about watching the attacks unfold from his window. I did a deep dive search for smaller details, like a 2001 computer science textbook from the New York Institute of Technology, to make sure the few lines of Roland's computer talk are accurate.

What is your writing process?
My writing process is like growing a garden. It starts as daydreaming about the seed of a story, something vague and far away that slowly gets closer and clearer as I think it over. A line of dialogue pops up, and then an amalgamation of tangled up emotions, experiences, and ideas. Characters begin to take shape, and after writing several terrible drafts, I finally get the location right, and the plot interesting enough. Then, I write more horrible scenes, until I get to a first draft that's readable. I prune back all the superfluous and ridiculous parts, weeding out everything that's nonessential. When it seems

healthy, I show it to readers I trust, who suggest cutting things out, and shifting placements around, until, hey, it looks pretty good. After a few extra versions, I settle on something I'm proud of and let the garden grow.

Shakespeare gave advice to the players in *Hamlet*; if you could give advice to your cast what would it be?
In true Shakespearian fashion, I cannot emphasize enough the importance of punctuation. It's written (as almost all plays are) with a natural speaking rhythm that indicates where to pause. Shakespearian actors know more than anyone that taking a break in a middle of line, dropping off the ends of phrases not on purpose, and emphasizing the non-active words can kill a scene. The power of lines lies in where you breathe and where you choose to power through without enough air in your lungs. That is what makes dynamic theatre.

How was the first production different from the vision that you created in your mind?
The first full production was vastly different, because I never imagined Jaime as a girl. In the original script, it was two brothers, but when we did the show for the New Works Festival at my high school, it ended up as me playing Roland's sister, instead of his brother. When I was rewriting the role for a female, I discovered how much I loved the new dynamic it created. Jaime's struggle to fill a maternal role, the weight of all the emotional labor she's doing, and her profound sense of failure at not being able to care for her brother fully felt incredibly authentic to me. In that production, they were half-siblings, which was later written out in following drafts, but the changing of Jacob to Jaime was a twist I fell in love with.

What's your favorite memory of the show?
My favorite memory was opening night of the first full production. In the end of the second scene, the lights are supposed to go down on Jaime still on stage with Roland,

because she's decided to stay with him. However, the light cue never came. One of us must have said a cue line a different way, or there was some mix up in the booth. Whatever happened, the two of us waited, sweating under the lights, waiting for them to go off. We sort of looked at each other in a panic and realized we'd have to end the scene off script. The actor playing Roland began quickly improvising more lines to keep the momentum going, but I figured they were waiting for me to leave before they ended the scene, and they couldn't just blackout while we were still talking. I said something along the lines of, "I'm sorry. I can't do this," and made a hasty exit. The lights went down and life went on. In later versions of the script, this improvised exit became the actual ending of the second scene and spawned the whole plotline of Jaime being absent on Christmas and the tension in the scene after. It was a happy accident that immensely improved the script overall!

About the Author

Rose Helsinger is a playwright and author from Florida. Her play, ***Albino Crocodile,*** was produced in New York and internationally by Missing Bolts Productions and NoPassport Theatre Alliance and Press, as part of ***After Orlando***, a collection of short plays written in response to the Pulse nightclub shooting. Additionally, Beth Marshall Presents, Kangagirl Productions, and the Orlando Shakespeare Theatre's annual Playfest have produced her plays. Her short stories, *You and Me and the End of the World* and *The Kitchen,* have been published in two of Page 15's annual anthologies. She is a member of Florida State University's class of 2021, majoring in Creative Writing and Education.

About YouthPLAYS

YouthPLAYS (www.youthplays.com) is a publisher of award-winning professional dramatists and talented new discoveries, each with an original theatrical voice, and all dedicated to expanding the vocabulary of theatre for young actors and audiences. On our website you'll find one-act and full-length plays and musicals for teen and pre-teen (and even college) actors, as well as duets and monologues for competition. Many of our authors' works have been widely produced at high schools and middle schools, youth theatres and other TYA companies, both amateur and professional, as well as at elementary schools, camps, churches and other institutions serving young audiences and/or actors worldwide. Most are intended for performance by young people, while some are intended for adult actors performing for young audiences.

YouthPLAYS was co-founded by professional playwrights Jonathan Dorf and Ed Shockley. It began merely as an additional outlet to market their own works, which included a substantial body of award-winning published and unpublished plays and musicals. Those interested in their published plays were directed to the respective publishers' websites, and unpublished plays were made available in electronic form. But when they saw the desperate need for material for young actors and audiences—coupled with their experience that numerous quality plays for young people weren't finding a home—they made the decision to represent the work of other playwrights as well. Dozens and dozens of authors are now members of the YouthPLAYS family, with scripts available both electronically and in traditional acting editions. We continue to grow as we look for exciting and challenging plays and musicals for young actors and audiences.

About ProduceaPlay.com

Let's put up a play! Great idea! But producing a play takes time, energy and knowledge. While finding the necessary time and energy is up to you, ProduceaPlay.com is a website designed to assist you with that third element: knowledge.

Created by YouthPLAYS' co-founders, Jonathan Dorf and Ed Shockley, ProduceaPlay.com serves as a resource for producers at all levels as it addresses the many facets of production. As Dorf and Shockley speak from their years of experience (as playwrights, producers, directors and more), they are joined by a group of award-winning theatre professionals and experienced teachers from the world of academic theatre, all making their expertise available for free in the hope of helping this and future generations of producers, whether it's at the school or university level, or in community or professional theatres.

The site is organized into a series of major topics, each of which has its own page that delves into the subject in detail, offering suggestions and links for further information. For example, Publicity covers everything from Publicizing Auditions to How to Use Social Media to Posters to whether it's worth hiring a publicist. Casting details Where to Find the Actors, How to Evaluate a Resume, Callbacks and even Dealing with Problem Actors. You'll find guidance on your Production Timeline, The Theater Space, Picking a Play, Budget, Contracts, Rehearsing the Play, The Program, House Management, Backstage, and many other important subjects.

The site is constantly under construction, so visit often for the latest insights on play producing, and let it help make your play production dreams a reality.

More from YouthPLAYS

Supermarket of Lost by Cassandra Hsiao

Drama. 15-20 minutes. 2 females, 1 male, 1 optional gender-flexible role.

Three young strangers collide at the Supermarket of Lost, a cosmic warehouse filled with the lost items of the world. As they explore the aisles and walk among people's memories, Austin, who is struggling with his past, connects with Hailee, who is struggling with her present. Accompanied by the young and spirited Violet, the two teens discover the difference between losing something and letting it go. Winner of the New Voices One-Act Competition for Young Playwrights.

An Avalanche of Murder by Matt Buchanan

Comic Mystery. 75-85 minutes. 8-12 females, 4-7 males (13-16 performers possible).

In this affectionate spoof of old-fashioned murder mysteries, the Hopkins family is trapped in a house by a freak avalanche, and they're dropping like flies. It's up to young Mary and Anthony to figure out who's killing them off one by one—and bragging about it on a dead phone—before there's nobody left.

Whirligig by John Newman

Drama. 65-75 minutes. 2-21 females, 3-21 males (5-30+ performers possible).

After Brent Bishop gets drunk at a party, causes a car accident, and kills a young woman, the aftermath of his actions overwhelms him. Desperate to find some way to undo the suffering he's caused, Brent accepts the challenge from the victim's mother: build four whirligigs in the corners of the country as memorials to her daughter. As he takes his journey, four individuals he never meets find their lives transformed by the whirligigs he builds. But will the teen be able to forgive his unforgivable mistake and move forward with his life?

Medusa's Tale by Carol S. Lashof
Drama. 25-35 minutes. 3-4 females, 2 males (5-6 performers possible).

Countless would-be heroes have tried to slay Medusa, the famous monster with snakes for hair, but each and every one has turned to stone, simply by meeting her gaze. The young Perseus is different, though. The Goddess Athena has given him a sword and shield and told him to beware of Medusa's tricks. But Perseus finds himself suddenly unprepared when Medusa's weapon of choice is the story of her life. Will Perseus stay true to his course and slay the monster, or will the humanity of Medusa's tale slay the hero?

Me, My Selfie & I by Jonathan Dorf
Dramedy. 40-50 minutes (flexible). 2-20 females, 2-20+ males (6-40+ performers possible).

We live in a world of social media, one in which we seem to be recording our every experience. But are we making memories or missing out on them? Through a series of scenes and monologues—everything from an accidental first date to a most unusual art exhibit to creating that last, best selfie—we meet a group of teens who are struggling to find the balance between documenting their lives and living them.

Cinderella: The Fairy Godmother's Tale by Louise Ricks
Comedy for Young Audiences. 30-40 minutes. 3-5 females, 1-3 males (6 performers total).

Everyone knows what happened at the ball, but no one knows what the Fairy Godmother had to do for Cinderella to win the prince's heart. Follow Phoebe, the newest Fairy Godmother-in-Training as she learns that real magic comes from hard work and faith in yourself. It's the classic story we all know and love, but with lots of laughter and a surprising magical twist!

Made in the USA
Columbia, SC
27 October 2021

47941992R00020